AF483077

Copyright © 2024 by Elizabeth A. Kipp

To request permission, contact kippysgirl@aol.com.

Cover and layout by Sarah Gargiulo
Illustrated by Paula Murphy

ISBN: 979-8-218-53600-8
Printed in the United States

Dedicated to my grandson, Jonathan Gargiulo,
who once realized that his Nana could do more
than just tell stories—she was also a real nurse,
offering care and comfort when he needed it most.

And to his little brother, Matthew,
whose joy and laughter fill my heart every day.

NANA NURSE

BY **Liz Kipp**

ILLUSTRATED BY **Paula Murphy**

My Nana loves me very much.

My Nana plays with me, with all of my favorite toys and games.

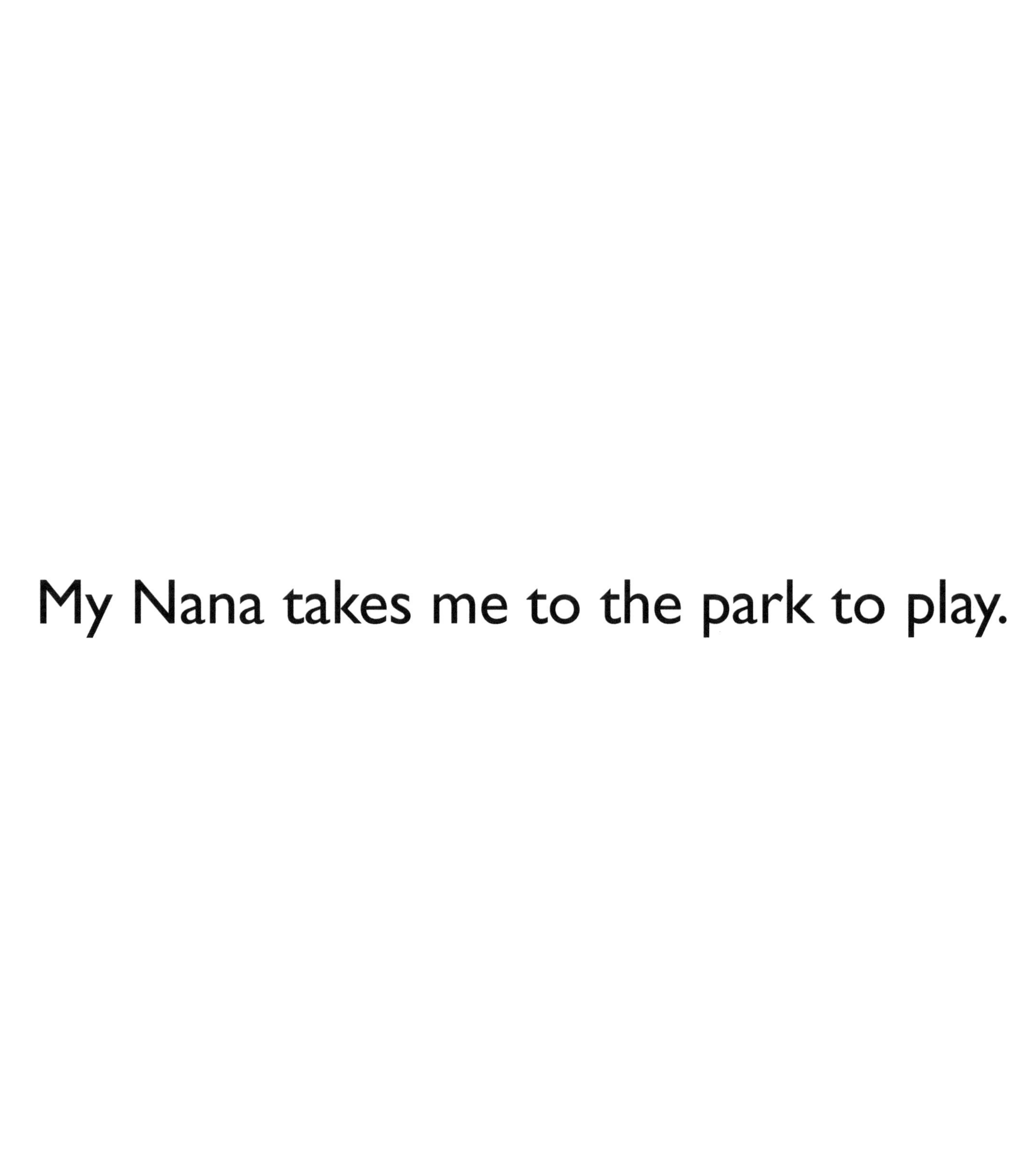

My Nana takes me to the park to play.

My Nana makes me healthy snacks
to eat when I am hungry.

My Nana reads to me at bedtime.

The Little Mouse
Captain Mouse

But I am a super lucky boy because my Nana is a nurse. A real Nurse!

When I get hurt, my Nana comforts me and always makes me feel better.

NANA NURSE

I am glad she is my Nana.
My Nana Nurse!

About the Author

Liz Kipp has dedicated her life to caring for others. She has been a nurse for over 52 years. She has spent the last 35 years working with Veterans at a Connecticut VA hospital, providing compassionate care to those who have served our country. Her passion for helping people inspired her to share her journey through stories like Nana Nurse, where she hopes to teach children the values of kindness, empathy, and healing.

In addition to her remarkable nursing career, Liz is a proud grandmother to four wonderful grandchildren who inspire her every day. They are her greatest joy and her motivation for continuing to make the world a better place, one patient—and one story—at a time.